"Roots" (Extended Edition Books 1-4)
by Vanco Kostadinov, Compiled by Petar Kostadinov
©2015

Roots

(Extended Edition Books 1-4)

By

Poetry Vanco Kostadinov

Compiled by Petar Kostadinov

(2015)

"Roots" (Extended Edition Books 1-4)
by Vanco Kostadinov, Compiled by Petar Kostadinov
©2015

Introduction

**These are the many poems that
fulfilled the heart of my father
Vanco Kostadinov.
He has that story in him to tell, that
will make you cry and laugh.**

-Author Petar Kostadinov

"Roots" (Extended Edition Books 1-4)
by Vanco Kostadinov, Compiled by Petar Kostadinov
©2015

Introduction

This book was published in 2013 only as "Roots". But Ever since my father Vanco Kostadinov passed away on December 1st, 2014 at the age 64, I had to bring out and finish his 4 small books into one, as he wanted me to. He quite made it to his birthday as his was on December 8th and born in 1950. He was a great man. Great father, grandfather and husband to my mother Jagotka. Also he was a great son, brother, brother-in law. He was great friend to his friends; always there when they needed him. You will find that in the poetry he has written and in mine which I have dedicated in my works. I have decided to finish translating his poetry, which would become much more bigger book as he asked me to do that for him when he saw the first edition and book 1 of 4.

So, in this version you will find the poetry from book 1 and it is extended through book 4. The separate editions are sold individually.

-Author Petar Kostadinov

"Roots" (Extended Edition Books 1-4)
by Vanco Kostadinov, Compiled by Petar Kostadinov
©2015

The cover picture plays significant role in this book. It is my great-grandfather Stojan Kostadinov.
This book is Part 1 of 4 poetry books separated as chapters of my father's life. Thanks again for reading my father's poetry and hopefully you will find something treasuring in your hearts as I did when he was telling them to me as a kid and then reading them when he wrote them.

-Author Petar Kostadinov of "Speechless Thunder" and many other works where you can purchase and read as well
through amazon.com
and barnesandnoble.com

"Roots" (Extended Edition Books 1-4)
by Vanco Kostadinov, Compiled by Petar Kostadinov
©2015

ISBN-13: 978-0692349809 (Custom)
ISBN-10: 0692349804

Published by www.pajkpublishing.com
Printed through createspace.com

FIRST PRINTING
U.S.A
© 2015 by Petar Kostadinov
©2015 by Vanco Kostadinov
All rights reserved. No part of this publication may be reproduced or transmitted in any form
by means, electronic or mechanical, including photocopy, recording, or any information storage and retrieval system, without permission in writing from the copyright owner.
In this book some of the poetry is fiction and some are non-fiction. Any resemblance to person, places, events, are pure coincidental.

Cover design by Petar Kostadinov

"Roots" (Extended Edition Books 1-4)
by Vanco Kostadinov, Compiled by Petar Kostadinov
©2015

"Roots" (Extended Edition Books 1-4)
by Vanco Kostadinov, Compiled by Petar Kostadinov
©2015

Contents   pg

Book 1

Summer	12
Cinder Blocks	14
Writing	16
I Am Sitting	18
Micho	19
Cadillac	21
Bank a House	23
Roots	24
House Divided	26
Old	27
Electricity-Slavica	28
Dirt	30
Efka	32

"Roots" (Extended Edition Books 1-4)
by Vanco Kostadinov, Compiled by Petar Kostadinov
©2015

Book 2

Black Bread	33
Cement Masons	36
Words Street	39
Division	42
Work	45
Jaundice	48
Healing Tea Plants	51
Vodno	52

Book 3

Spear	55
Discussions	57
Cold-Flu	58
Grandmother	59
Grandchildren	60
Childhood	61
Snails	64
Wool	66

"Roots" (Extended Edition Books 1-4)
by Vanco Kostadinov, Compiled by Petar Kostadinov
©2015

Book 4

Milk Factory	67
A House	69
Wegmans-U.S.A.	70
Changes	71
Przhdevo-Watermelon	73
Harship's in Przhdevo	75
Przhedevo	77
Kolbasi and Slama	78
Pelister's Lake	80
Uphill On Przhdevo's Hilltop	82
Eating, Eating	84
Hunter	86
Huge Bad Rock	88
War 1999	90
Mississippi River -Lake	92

"Roots" (Extended Edition Books 1-4)
by Vanco Kostadinov, Compiled by Petar Kostadinov
©2015

Snow 29/12/1998   94
New York 1998   95

"Roots" (Extended Edition Books 1-4)
by Vanco Kostadinov, Compiled by Petar Kostadinov
©2015

Book 1

Summer

Sokol I ride that white horse
Besides that Vardar River
I swim in the streams
And they twirl summer water
Nobody lends me a hand
I came out startled
When luck desires
Afterwards without any Time

"Roots" (Extended Edition Books 1-4)
by Vanco Kostadinov, Compiled by Petar Kostadinov
©2015

A Horse bangs
me on rocky
fields
It pulls me
It drags me
It cuts me
My grandpa with
his magical
power
He heals me

"Roots" (Extended Edition Books 1-4)
by Vanco Kostadinov, Compiled by Petar Kostadinov
©2015

Cinder Blocks

Cinder blocks in
Ushici, ushici,
Forest, forest,
forest
Does not have a
thought
All summer long
I was
making cinder
blocks

"Roots" (Extended Edition Books 1-4)
by Vanco Kostadinov, Compiled by Petar Kostadinov
©2015

And more from
the neighbors
and great souls
I am building a
home and a house
I am building it
for happiness and
luck
To have
No one today is
thinking that my
house
And river is their
luck.

Writing

I am writing so it
can be easier
For me to breath
My pencil is
writing
my brain is
Erasing
Easing, writing
Written
something
Serious

What is said
sweeter
Someday sweeter
Once bad
My pencil began
"to act like
Tosho"

"Roots" (Extended Edition Books 1-4)
by Vanco Kostadinov, Compiled by Petar Kostadinov
©2015

I Am Sitting

I am sitting and
waiting
In waiting I turn
into stone
But they say
You have to wait
with patience
And I will fall
Asleep

"Roots" (Extended Edition Books 1-4)
by Vanco Kostadinov, Compiled by Petar Kostadinov
©2015

Micho

Our friend Micho
From Skopje
In his hands he had an arrow
And he smiles bless fully
When he speaks he makes
Everyone laugh

But he never makes
mistakes
And his words flowed
in song

Cadillac

People drive wild cars
Some go on walking
Some drive bicycles
Heart and soul it hurts
Neither I have a ford
Neither I have a
Chevy
What kind of God is
this?
Is he pleading helping
the poor

"Roots" (Extended Edition Books 1-4)
by Vanco Kostadinov, Compiled by Petar Kostadinov
©2015

The rich do not care
The poor their soul
hurts
Heavy worked out
souls
Their heaviness is
draining them
They cannot breathe
Their body aches and
falls into pieces.

Bank a House

Bank a house of cinder blocks is built
Builder is constructing it
Some throw cinder blocks around
Some catch those cinder blocks
Above
Sunny days are rising

Roots

A field for a house
Roots are pulled out
Bones from the dead
Are coming in light
Soldiers have died
here
These are their graves
For peace they fought
Hands they washed
Such a luck

What kind of unlucky day
This is
What is that?
Lucky in a sown bag
For some lucky
For some unlucky
No matter for some how
Is written
For some, is very warm
For some very cold

House Divided

Somebody wants to
Divide this house
Money has to be paid
Each month
Somebody's mind
Is twirling
Are there any good reasons?
Are there any solid grounds?

Brotherly, brotherly, brotherly
Brotherly House to be divided
With happy great ideas

"Roots" (Extended Edition Books 1-4)
by Vanco Kostadinov, Compiled by Petar Kostadinov
©2015

Old

When you are old you feel
sick
The old age makes it that
way
Some with pain some with
nerves
Some eat a lot some
refuse to eat
a whole lot
work my son, work my
dear
but it does not seem to be
wanting to work
a lot I want free Saturday

"Roots" (Extended Edition Books 1-4)
by Vanco Kostadinov, Compiled by Petar Kostadinov
©2015

Electricity-Slavica

Bricks of stone
Are set to built
Very hot summer
On the soul humid
hot
There is no water this
morning
Bathroom without
water
She goes in the
bathroom
Without checking if
there is water

For her to wash up
her hands
From the bathroom
she screams
She holds tight with
her hands
The boiler
I run real quickly
I break down the
door
I turn off the chord
from the outlet
she is now save
because I saved her
life

"Roots" (Extended Edition Books 1-4)
by Vanco Kostadinov, Compiled by Petar Kostadinov
©2015

Dirt

Digging if a land
The land is being
washed
A dirt for bricks to be
built
Bare feet stepping
The arms are lifting a
shovel
Dirt, dirt, dirt
Quality workmanship
Dirt

Masonry
subcontractors is
making it
To be set in wooden
cart

"Roots" (Extended Edition Books 1-4)
by Vanco Kostadinov, Compiled by Petar Kostadinov
©2015

Efka

Subcontractors are
building a house
She preparing food
Bringing pans
With very hot
mancha soups
She is bringing it up
the hilltop

"Roots" (Extended Edition Books 1-4)
by Vanco Kostadinov, Compiled by Petar Kostadinov
©2015

Book 2

"Roots" (Extended Edition Books 1-4)
by Vanco Kostadinov, Compiled by Petar Kostadinov
©2015

Black Bread

In a hot furnace
A black bread is
baking.
For a whole week
In a peaceful glory
The first two days
the black bread
I loved
And afterward
I broke it on stones
Because from soft
became hard.

"Roots" (Extended Edition Books 1-4)
by Vanco Kostadinov, Compiled by Petar Kostadinov
©2015

I gave it to my dog
Murgo. Murgo barked
and barked.
Yelled and yelled.
He woke up easily in
the woods, did not give
us easily to sleep
In the old country town,
Graeshnica under the
beauty of "Grandma
Mountain"
There is Clear,
Mountain Pelister's
Lake
Pears, cherries, apples,
Nuts, peaches...
Fields full filled with
vegetables and flowers
For some heaven for
some hell

"Roots" (Extended Edition Books 1-4)
by Vanco Kostadinov, Compiled by Petar Kostadinov
©2015

An old town for
younger generation
joyful
Today
Macedonian-Christians
keep on leaving in
distant lands for better
life
For white bread
For peace
For happiness

"Roots" (Extended Edition Books 1-4)
by Vanco Kostadinov, Compiled by Petar Kostadinov
©2015

Cement Masons

I am bringing buckets
Full with concrete water
Mason workers with great minds
Mason workers skinny as bones all of them thorn to pieces from sweat

All of their faces dried up, their mouths and lips too
I carry dirty not washed buckets that are heavy

Cement Mason as I am working twelve hours hours I steer
And I carry dried small piece of bread in a small little bag made with

peppers

Masons yell
Child, Child
Bring us some more
Concrete

I tell them
Here I am
I am bringing you
More concrete
My feet are bear
They are building,
Building, not a day off
From school, or vacation
There is no Mountainous
beauty

There are no lakes to
enjoy

"Roots" (Extended Edition Books 1-4)
by Vanco Kostadinov, Compiled by Petar Kostadinov
©2015

Concrete Mason
Bring us some healing
Flowers
On Pelister and Pelagonije
He is landscaping

We had one Kid
That for some reason
He did not want to go with
us

"Roots" (Extended Edition Books 1-4)
by Vanco Kostadinov, Compiled by Petar Kostadinov
©2015

Words Street

In An Old Jewish
House my twin brothers
Were born
It was very rough times
My parents were paying
rent
Water from distance we
bring
In a red heavy bucket
I was heavy like that
Bucket
My feet were shoe-less
No Nike sneakers, no
Reebok shirts
Sharp plants, stones my
feet are cutting
In the field yard goats
and pigs

"Roots" (Extended Edition Books 1-4)
by Vanco Kostadinov, Compiled by Petar Kostadinov
©2015

Winter times freezing
winds erasing and cutting
The pigs are screaming
The bathroom is farther
away in the yard
Freezing cold dried air
There is not a drop of hot
Warm water bath

Once a week I take a bath
In a sink
All day long I run in the
streets and play
There is no need to worry
Times, Old Times, Bad
Times
At the park in Bitola, 1959
On the street Number 1
Today I dream about my
childhood
The dream from dream

"Roots" (Extended Edition Books 1-4)
by Vanco Kostadinov, Compiled by Petar Kostadinov
©2015

Is awaking me
Today 1999 I live in
Rochester, America,
State of NY.
Today someone still want
to Judge me, without fault,
there is not a word of
saying.

"Roots" (Extended Edition Books 1-4)
by Vanco Kostadinov, Compiled by Petar Kostadinov
©2015

Division

Divide from each other
Divide from each other
Father in law
Mother in law
Brother in law
Sister in law

Life does not run
Smoothly like honey
Grandpa Sweet
Grandma Frog
Understanding,
Misunderstanding
Through the divided
house someone is
stepping on

Someone is wanting

"Roots" (Extended Edition Books 1-4)
by Vanco Kostadinov, Compiled by Petar Kostadinov
©2015

The whole world
Life continues
Someone does not
Give in
Someone still
Continues
Division, division
Everybody was mad
Everybody argued each
other

"Roots" (Extended Edition Books 1-4)
by Vanco Kostadinov, Compiled by Petar Kostadinov
©2015

Work

There is no Job
I keep on spitting on
The streets
I keep on eating
Seeds
I am going to leave
From here and go
To America
There are Jobs
Over there
I came to America
And there are jobs
I work from Monday
to Sunday night and
day
There is no break
I work for something
But at the end there

is no money again
There is nothing left
Just paying bills
Nothing is important
But that is life.

Jaundice

My mother is
throwing up
She has a headache
And with a headband
She heals her head
She is throwing up
Yellowish mucus
I am bringing her
Empty bucket
To help her out
I wash it, I scrub it
I offer her something
to eat and juice to
drink
But she does not
want to

Everything makes
her sick
Her stomach gets
All tangled up
In knots
Very awful migraine
I go over to check on
her to see if she is
still breathing
I asked her to get up
She says to me
"no, no, no,"
My thoughts were
That she was going
to die
But the very next day
She gets up and
begins to work
Around the house
To look after it

"Roots" (Extended Edition Books 1-4)
by Vanco Kostadinov, Compiled by Petar Kostadinov
©2015

She is fighting
Against the poorness
And Homelessness
Not to be

Healing Tea Plants

Early in the morning
"Get up my Son,
We are going in
Pelagonija
With metal big
combs to pick up
Healing Tea Plants."
Big bags are full
Businessman are
purchasing them
They pay us money,
Money, but I hardly
Could see them,
something to be
made. Everyone is
asking a lot of loved
ones. Migraines

"Roots" (Extended Edition Books 1-4)
by Vanco Kostadinov, Compiled by Petar Kostadinov
©2015

Vodno

Dry Hill
They say it is Vodno
There is no river
stream
There is no lake
There is not a great
Comfy Place to sit
Every body goes on
their weekends to
Vodno
To feel healed
To feel straight
alright not a pain in
my body or mind
To receive a sports
wooden stick

"Roots" (Extended Edition Books 1-4)
by Vanco Kostadinov, Compiled by Petar Kostadinov
©2015

Book 3

"Roots" (Extended Edition Books 1-4)
by Vanco Kostadinov, Compiled by Petar Kostadinov
©2015

Spear

This is Main Place
But it is very tight
Skopje, Vardar
Skopje's Walls
Not a paper
I keep on studying
Learning
Around Skopje only
peace

Learning, learning,
Learning
My head keeps on
buzzing

There is no lunch
Only parties
There is only
Freedom
Spear, spear, spear
We were looking for
Skopje
But we found it in
Another Spear.

Discussions

I have many to write
Different teams and
thoughts

In my body I have
many pains

Penicillin helps
It heals me little
It kills the Bacteria
For my body not to
Be in half
Many discussions
Many ideas
It opened every line

"Roots" (Extended Edition Books 1-4)
by Vanco Kostadinov, Compiled by Petar Kostadinov
©2015

Cold-Flu

Cold-Flu, simple Flu
In my throat shallow
I keep on choking
Coughing
Keep on thinking
On beautiful cleaner
Cold, cold
My nose is running,
running, running
There is no such a
cure that can heal me
Viruses, viruses,
viruses

Grandmother

It seems she cares
a lot
All day long
She thinks about her
Grandchildren
In Prilep they work
hard and carry a lot
of plantation on their
back so they can sell
them to build a
bigger house
For better life of their
family

"Roots" (Extended Edition Books 1-4)
by Vanco Kostadinov, Compiled by Petar Kostadinov
©2015

Grandchildren

Two granddaughters
Two Grandsons
Grandchildren smarter
Wiser
I find myself in a strange
Hardship
I watch over them
I take care of them

Childhood

Street Word Number One
I am heading to school
Kole Kaninski
I pass by the river
Kurdeles
I am reading my Bukvar
from school
For breakfast I am
drinking milk
Milk that was send over
from United States
Milk made in Powder
My Teacher Rada
"Drink, Eat, children"
She says.
"After breakfast, we will
read the Bukvar,"
My reading is tough

"Roots" (Extended Edition Books 1-4)
by Vanco Kostadinov, Compiled by Petar Kostadinov
©2015

At home we had homework, I hardly
Finish them. I am frustrated with my parents
My mother keeps on telling me to do the homework.
For things to finish up
To bring water from the faucet in a red big bucket
Heavier than I am
Faucet that is far in distance by the Factory Svilara.
Then to feed the pigs
Chickens to check on them to see if there are any eggs. If they have any eggs not to let them out so they don't lay them outside

Plus I had to take care of my two twin brothers
My mother had migraines
Two twin brothers with different faces, had to give them milk in a baby bottles. One keeps on taking it from the other. My mother always with headaches. I have to help her out. Because I love her.

Snails

We get up
Early in the morning
We go to gather
snails
Beautiful cute snails
I don't want to get up
Early in the morning
I don't to gather
snails today
I am going to
America
Land of opportunity
Maybe my soul will
Ache for my home
land

"Roots" (Extended Edition Books 1-4)
by Vanco Kostadinov, Compiled by Petar Kostadinov
©2015

My soul will
hiccup, hiccup,
hiccup
Snails that are slimy,
slimy.

Wool

White shaved wool
Diseases Flea is
catching on
To them
There is no hay
For them to eat
Meat full with mold
Wool going bad
Wool are dying
Goats keep on crying
There is death
everywhere

Milk Factory

instead of white Milk
Blue, Blue, Blue
Milk that was stirred
in with unclean
pasteurized kind
Too much of that
In the Unclean metal
holding tanks
In a very low
temperature
People keep on
yelling, screaming
The children have
Diarrhea

The old retired folks
Are holding money
in their hands

A House

I did not built a
house but bought
Apartment
My children need
more food
I go and bring them
some
My wife is pregnant
My children are
thirsty
My wife is hard
worker
For love of us
She is very thirsty

"Roots" (Extended Edition Books 1-4)
by Vanco Kostadinov, Compiled by Petar Kostadinov
©2015

Wegmans-U.S.A.

A huge Grocery Store
Carries everything
All kinds of variety of
foods buying from bread,
vegetable, fruits, meat, ice
cream,
My feet are tired
I no longer can walk
Need some rest

Changes

I lost But I gained a lot
I left my Birth Country
Macedonia
I flew in a bigger beautiful
land United States Of
America
The changes I made on
time
I saw many cultures,
religions, languages.

I am
Worker on many fields
Businessman, creative
guy,

Hard worker with physical strength

I hope I still have time
To take another road
For better or worse
For newer beliefs
For new excitements
For new spending's
New thinking
New heartbreak
New special foods
New drinks
New fashions
New TV shows
New, new, dramas.

"Roots" (Extended Edition Books 1-4)
by Vanco Kostadinov, Compiled by Petar Kostadinov
©2015

Przhdevo Watermelon

I am looking for water
I am looking for juice
There is no water nor juice
Watermelon, grapefruit,
there is everywhere
In Przhdev's Climate
Very hot and dry air
There is no cold water
Very few wells
Vardar's streams
We are fueling on olive oil,
water and garlic.

"Roots" (Extended Edition Books 1-4)
by Vanco Kostadinov, Compiled by Petar Kostadinov
©2015

There is no meat
There is no sugar
There is no flour
Peppers, it was poverty

When I was growing up
Throughout my childhood

Hardship's in Przhdevo

We are going with my
grandpa Kiro in tiredness
In Well fixed up patched
up car he is driving us
Sokol White Horse he is
pulling us
Through the riding the
tiredness evolved
Sokol started to run right
The car started to jump
My grandpa started yelling
"Ou, Ou, Ou,"
With hold up and scare
He stopped the horse
Sokol

Now quiet, and my
grandpa with quite voice
calm him down
He saved our lives.

Przhdevo

Village, village that is happy
Happy and joyful
Only the men
Drink white wine
Women do not drink
Women clean up
Men do not
Dry, dry, dry
Not a drop of rain
Has fallen
Everywhere spikes of leaves

"Roots" (Extended Edition Books 1-4)
by Vanco Kostadinov, Compiled by Petar Kostadinov
©2015

Kolbasi and Slama

Kolbasi, Kolbasi
Empty tables
Kolbasi kolbasi
Full rich tables
They drink wine
They eat
There is no theater
Business busy work
There is none free
Saturday
Bare feet, bare feet, bare feet.
Mowing, mowing, mowing
Rain is falling on the mountains

Fields and grass

Grain and chaff
Horses keep on working
the fields, grains and
slama hay
Which you cannot see
That at home.

"Roots" (Extended Edition Books 1-4)
by Vanco Kostadinov, Compiled by Petar Kostadinov
©2015

Pelister's Lake

It was summer
They send me
In the village
Pelister village
Graeshnica
River beautiful
River Kishovska
The streams were
Blocking with rocks
And bazje
I am catching fish
From underneath those rock
With bare hands
Nothing is hurting me
I am eating cherries, pears
The fish that I was catching

"Roots" (Extended Edition Books 1-4)
by Vanco Kostadinov, Compiled by Petar Kostadinov
©2015

My grandmother Cveta made them for me on a grilled stove
I was a child I was very happy, with joyful heart
Sometimes I was out of control playing around

"Roots" (Extended Edition Books 1-4)
by Vanco Kostadinov, Compiled by Petar Kostadinov
©2015

Uphill on Przhdevo's Tophill

Very heavy summer
Very hot
We are walking without shoes bare naked feet
The sun keeps on burning
Us and every which way
Very sharp leaves on the view
Very dry and cold water in the well
I am holding that and bringing it in an old leaves
Closed nicely
People are bringing peppers

"Roots" (Extended Edition Books 1-4)
by Vanco Kostadinov, Compiled by Petar Kostadinov
©2015

I am running through the
aches over to Vardar, and
go swimming
Sun is burning me
The river Vardar is murky
Water keeps on running

Eating, Eating

Eat, Eat, Eat,
All of the time
I feel like throwing up
I feel like I have to
Take it from my mouth
Like its going to fall out
I am spitting it out,
throwing up, I am
hiccuping.
I am eating food with
force
But can't eat everything
I need some help
Or something else
The food is catching on
my throat
I feel like I am going to
die
I feel the world had ended

"Roots" (Extended Edition Books 1-4)
by Vanco Kostadinov, Compiled by Petar Kostadinov
©2015

I feel like I am sick from cancer
Thinking that something
Will keep me going
Keep on eating and
Have a good night sleep
To feel better
To be happy
To be relaxed
To be normal
To be beautiful, godly, Sane

Hunter

The Hunter goes to catch
something in the woods
Does not have pain in his
body, always praying,
something to hunt
He comes to many roads
Uphill taller, downhill
wider
Must be running
To find wild animals
But he comes to Mara
And they start to argue
She is arguing, yelling
Because she is worried
A friend that is thirsty
Friend that is hard worker
What she sees is that he

caught a pig that he battled
for them to eat
The hunter is not anymore
in trouble

"Roots" (Extended Edition Books 1-4)
by Vanco Kostadinov, Compiled by Petar Kostadinov
©2015

Huge Bad Rock

Pelister's part
When you pull it apart
You will find
Lake of Prespa

Aegean Macedonia
Lerin Watered
Beautiful land
Beautiful sightseeing
Always tight
Always alive with music
Balkans great light
Balkans great beauty

"Roots" (Extended Edition Books 1-4)
by Vanco Kostadinov, Compiled by Petar Kostadinov
©2015

Where there is loudness
We all ask for peace,
peace, peace, and
treasured streamlines

"Roots" (Extended Edition Books 1-4)
by Vanco Kostadinov, Compiled by Petar Kostadinov
©2015

War 1999

Local Wars unexpected wars
With Tanks, Airplanes, Nuclear Bombs,
Rockets keep on flying everywhere,
Innocent People scattered everywhere
And children are suppose to live in peace to play with their toys, dolls
From Baba Meca,
Please Stop all of the Wars
Let's live in Peace and safety
Stop all of that Rape
Stop all the religion hate

"Roots" (Extended Edition Books 1-4)
by Vanco Kostadinov, Compiled by Petar Kostadinov
©2015

among each other.
Please think about it
What is going on here
God will have to come and
stop this madness and hate
Among us humans

"Roots" (Extended Edition Books 1-4)
by Vanco Kostadinov, Compiled by Petar Kostadinov
©2015

Mississippi River-Lake

Huge, wide, blurry
river that gives hope
River that takes stable
River that speaks about
Danger
River that hopes for love
I went to see it
Starry, Shinny, Godly
River you must be careful
Not to fall and get hurt
River that is incredible
River for the Tourists to
see this beauty
That shows love to
everyone

"Roots" (Extended Edition Books 1-4)
by Vanco Kostadinov, Compiled by Petar Kostadinov
©2015

This old River that not anyone can see but must go travel to see

Snow 29/12/1998

Northern Snow Northern
Winds blowing erasing
You can hardly breathe
Everything is frozen
We are close to Alaska
We need masks on our mouth
To breathe warmer
To breathe peaceful
To breathe easier
The heart does not beat
Heart beating drums

Everywhere snow and Ice
Wind with Godly sounds

New York 1998

City that does not sleep
Place that all the time
drinks parties all night
long
That is why everyone
Asks for something
In the Restaurants and
Bars
When you walk on the
Streets I felt dizzy
That is that
I wanted to see that beauty
And I saw it
Two ways, One way
streets

"Roots" (Extended Edition Books 1-4)
by Vanco Kostadinov, Compiled by Petar Kostadinov
©2015

I love that place
It reminds me of my
younger years how life use

to be before I got married
Wherever is happiness
Then there is great joy
The heart is like thunder

"Roots" (Extended Edition Books 1-4)
by Vanco Kostadinov, Compiled by Petar Kostadinov
©2015

To know more about the Author visit;

http://www.amazon.com/Vanco-Kostadinov/e/B00J1UGRUC/ref=sr_ntt_srch_1nk_1?qid=1418802861&sr=8-1

www.barnesandnoble.com

www.pajkpublishing.com

Visit your local library too.

You may also order his books from your local stores.

"Roots" (Extended Edition Books 1-4)
by Vanco Kostadinov, Compiled by Petar Kostadinov
©2015

Notes

"Roots" (Extended Edition Books 1-4)
by Vanco Kostadinov, Compiled by Petar Kostadinov
©2015

Notes

"Roots" (Extended Edition Books 1-4)
by Vanco Kostadinov, Compiled by Petar Kostadinov
©2015

Notes

"Roots" (Extended Edition Books 1-4)
by Vanco Kostadinov, Compiled by Petar Kostadinov
©2015

Notes

www.ingramcontent.com/pod-product-compliance
Lightning Source LLC
Chambersburg PA
CBHW071311060426
42444CB00034B/1938